RidiCulOus RhymEs

By Peter Le Cheminant

Illustrations by Trudie Shannon

Peter Le Cheminant was born in Guernsey where his family line goes back to 1636. His mother 'bolted' when he was eight thus freeing him of the obligations of one half of the Fifth Commandment and at a stroke conferring on him what at the time he perceived to be the benefits of a youth untrammeled by maternal diktat. He passed into the Royal Air Force College Cranwell aged 18 in 1938 and was commissioned in 1939. He retired as an Air Chief Marshal in 1979 as Deputy Commander in Chief of Allied Forces Central Europe. Of his 41 years' service some 20 were spent abroad and, as a pilot, he flew 73 different aircraft types from biplane trainers through wartime tactical bombers to postwar flying boats and helicopters, jet bombers and Mach 2 fighters. On retirement from the Royal Air Force he was appointed Lieutenant-Governor of Guernsey and its Dependencies by Her Majesty, the first Guernseyman to be so honoured for some 600 years.

Peter Le Cheminant has always enjoyed writing. He won first prize in an essay competition at the age of eight, wrote extensively on service matters during his working life being three times winner of the Royal United Services Institute Gold Medal Essay Prize. He has published two novels and an autobiography about his years in the Royal Air Force. He wrote these rhymes in 1953–54 when he was a Wing Commander on the Joint Planning Staff, partly to amuse his younger daughter (the subject of Younger Female) and partly to have an alternative to *Pooh Bear* and *Barbar the Elephant*.

In retirement Le Cheminant plays a good deal of golf and lives in an old farmhouse where he panders to his two cats, spends a good deal of time wondering whether it is too early for a gin and tonic and struggling to recall the names of his eight great-grandchildren.

Predictably his favourite author is P. G. Wodehouse.

ABOUT THE ILLUSTRATOR

Trudie Shannon is an artist and poet born and educated in Guernsey. Born in 1956, she held her first one woman exhibition in 1982 and has shown her work consistently since then including shows in Northern Ireland and England. Her most recent exhibition *Inside Out* was shown successfully in both Jersey and Guernsey in 2004. She is now planning her next which will take place in France in 2006. She has also had a small collection of her poetry published.

THE HIPPOPOTAMUS

Some Hippopotami

Are very often shy

About their bottomi.

If a hippopotamus was a hippopotamass
Would it then be bottom of the class?

If I was an Ox

I'd sit in a box
My tail curled under me in a loop
So no-one could make it into soup

THE CUCKOO

Do cuckoos give a thought at all
To why their parents seem so small?

SIR PERRIVALE TWANK

Sir Perrivale Twank
Was a bit of a crank
He liked mustard with porridge
Kept bees in his bed
And every third Sunday he tattooed his head.

Sir Perrivale's wife
Was the bane of his life
She bathed in his cider
And varnished his clothes
And to make matters worse she ate with her toes.

Sir Perrivale's son
Did things which aren't done
He kept frogs in his topper
Cocked snooks at the Bart
And lived on pease pudding and cranberry tart.

Sir Perrivale's daughter
(A ton and a quarter)
Was tedious and dull
Her solitary vice
Was serving fresh strawberries and ice cream to mice.

Their friends said 'My dear
Yes, they're terribly queer
Quite harmless of course
But definitely cranks
You really don't know where you are with the Twanks'.

Sir Perrivale view'd
His intolerable brood
He pondered that verdict
And thought it was right
So he banished the whole twanking lot from his sight.

YOUNG MALE

I'm fed up with stories of Pussy and Bunny
Of fat little bears who are too fond of honey
Of rats who are rascals and owls who are wise
Of fat little kittens with googly eyes.
Give me stories of space ships and nuclear cars
Owned by mechanical men from Mars

I don't believe in fairies, in bogey-men or witches
In demons, giants or goblins with their little pointy ears
I'm too grown-up for that stuff which is only good for children
Who are very young and simple and still play with Teddy Bears

But do you believe in vampires, in ghoulish grinning zombies
In ghastly green-faced ghosties with the Hangman's Mark?
I don't think I do really, though I'm not entirely certain –
I'm not the least bit certain in winter after dark.

YOUNGER FEMALE

I'm growing up. I'll be seven next yere
Orltho I can't spel
Very wel
I can do tens and yewnits and make cloze for my bere
Have you ever been to Tralfgar Sqeer?

I've got a skool hat. I like my new frok
Its fewsher and pink
I think
I can do five times tabel and tell time by the clok
Have you got a nice new mashintok?

I've got a grate-arnt, she seems very old
Bout hundred and four
Or more
I make my dolls drink whiskey - they never catch cold
Do you do x-actly what youre told?

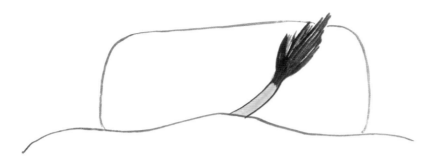

When a Giraffe gets into bed

I wonder where he puts his head?

THE PELICAN

The pelican is a handsome bird
Whom all admire but upon my word
Have you ever seen the Pelicant?
No? Well don't. Looks like my aunt!

THE NEWT

When a Newt's not quite as young as he was
I feel very sorry for him because
It must give you a very nasty jolt
When you suddenly find that you're an Oldt.

FIFI-LE-MOKO

I once knew a poodle of high degree
Who wanted to marry a Pekinee
She was modishly groomed, had a most refined bark
And she pranced like a pedigree lamb in the park
She had excellent manners and manicured nails
And although she was French she didn't eat snails
Her looks were exotic, her hairstyle the vogue
As an added attraction she woofed with a brogue
She was conscious of fashion and all that that meant
And had bottles and bottles of best doggie scent
She tried being roguish and tried being meek
But she couldn't attract that inscrutable Peke
Which was hardly surprising – poor Fifi-le-Moko
She wasn't all black – her tail, it was COCOA!

THE CHIMPANZEE

If a Chimpanzee of the very first clutch
Had not come from Africa but had been Dutch
It might have been called, yes, now let me see
Not a Chimp, but a Chimpanzuiderzee.
Had it dressed not in fur but in a zoot suit
It might have been called a Chimpanzuiderzeezoot.

KING JOHN'S CROWN

King John had some funny ways, there's little doubt of that
When he went to bed one night he wore his silk top hat
He also wore his trousers, which looked a little daft
But they were better than his night shirt at keeping out the draught

He got up in the morning and went to greet the Queen
Who said 'Lawk a mercy Johnathon you're not fit to be seen
Now take your hat and trousers off, and wash, and clean your tooth
I don't know what you're thinking of, I really don't, forsooth.'

King John was very downcast as he wandered off to wash
He didn't feel like bathing as he'd lost his mackintosh.
He sloshed some water on his face (but no behind his ears)
And by the time he'd finished he was very near to tears

She didn't like his trousers, and she didn't like his hat
(He didn't like hers either, but he daren't tell her that)
What could he do to please her, he wondered with a frown?
Ah yes, of course, the very thing – he'd polish up his crown

His crown was in the counting house, high above the moat
And before he started up the stairs he donned his ermine coat
It was tight around the middle (he was getting rather fat)
But he looked a kingly figure, for he still retained his hat

He pattered up the staircase with his brasso tin and rag
His button stick and brushes in his little khaki bag
Intent to make his crown shine (it had not been cleaned before)
But lay rather green and tarnished with the lumber on the floor

When out of breath and panting to the counting-house he came
He found its solid oaken door set in its oaken frame
Was locked and barred and bolted, as tight shut as could be
(A notice by a scurvy knave said 'Sorry, gone to tea').

King John was disappointed and he said 'Oh dearie me
How very, very tiresome, I shall have to fetch the key
Oh bother, what a nuisance, it's such a long way down
And I did so want to polish up my crown'.

He pattered down the stairs as fast as he could go
And just outside a scullions' room he stubbed his little toe
Being very conscious of what a well dressed King should wear
It made him blush bright scarlet to find his feet were bare.

He hunted all around his room and underneath his bed
And couldn't find his boots or shoes but found his spurs instead
He didn't want to wear his socks (he knew that with top hats
The better dressed amongst the Kings invariably wore spats)

He looked into the mirror when thus attired and dressed
And in spite of what the Queen might say he knew he looked his best
The castle roof was leaky and he thought it looked like rain
So he took his brolly with him when he started back again

When he unlocked the oaken door and tried to throw it wide
He saw he'd have to draw the bolt ere he could pass inside
He pushed and pulled and heaved and strained but couldn't make it move
And saw on looking closer it was rusted in its groove.

When he tried once more in vain he said with a grimace
'There's only one thing for it, I shall have to fetch my mace
Oh bother, what a nuisance, it's such a long way down
And I did so want to polish up my crown'.

He hurried to his room again and got his mace so trusty
(It was a very handsome one, although a trifle rusty)
He had to take his Kingly shield and wear a chain-mail vest
(King's can't use their maces unless they're properly dressed)

The simple King set off again, his step was quite light-hearted
He knew that when he'd blipped that bolt he really should get started
He didn't think of breakfast or going into town
The only thing he wanted was to polish up his crown

He leant his shield against the wall and lifted up his mace
With mighty swing he bopped that bolt and knocked it out of place
And when he found an iron bar still held the door tight shut
King John lost his temper (and I think he said tut tut).

To break that bar he saw he would need at least a dozen thwacks
He said 'There's nothing for it, I must fetch my battle axe
Of bother, what a nuisance, it's such a long way down
And I did so want to polish up my crown.'

Then axe in hand he left his room all eager for his quest
His conscience spoke to him and said 'King John get properly dressed.'
He knew a self-respecting King who cared for the conventions
Should always wear a sword as well whatever his intentions)

He clanked and clattered up the stairs to reach that room on high
And though you may not think it he never heaved a sigh
He was happy, he was laughing, he didn't wear a frown
'Cause he knew he'd soon be able to polish up his crown.

WHAT I WANT TO BE

Sometimes I think I'd like to be a soldier on a horse
Then I might become a General and live on Worcester Sauce
And I would bristle my moustache
Pretending to be stern and harsh
And everyone I saw would say
The General's very fierce today.

Sometimes I think I'd like to be a sailor dressed in blue
Then I might become an Admiral with face of purply hue
I wouldn't need to stamp or shout
I'd simply make my eyes pop out
And every sailor good or bad
Would say the Admiral's hopping mad.

Sometimes I think I'd like to be a doctor so sedate
I'd have a stethoscope and bag and polish my brass plate
To cure you of all kind of ills
I'd give you funny little pills
I'd wear a top hat with a shine
And practice saying ninety nine.

Sometimes I think I'd like to be the driver of a train
So I could drive to John O'Groats and then drive back again
I'd have a mate to shovel coal
Into the engine's boiler hole
I'd wear an oily mackintosh
And wouldn't often have to wash.
(But now its changed and steams no more
It's lost a lot of its allure.)

Sometimes I think I'd like to be a Bandit fierce and brave
I might live in a forest or I might live in a cave
I'd have a gun and lots of knives
And maybe I'd have several wives
I'd terrorise all other men
And wouldn't go to bed till ten.

Sometimes I think I'd like to be the head of Scotland Yard
Then criminals would find that I was ruthless, cold and hard
I'd break up all the smuggling rings
And international other things
Which bad men seem to think are fun
And judges say should not be done.

Sometimes I think I'd like to be a super sort of spy
I'd change my voice and wear a beard and be called 'x' or 'y'
I'd write in very secret ink
And always have champagne to drink
The Queen would send for me and say
'We want the plans so start today'.

Of all the things I've thought about I think that probably
A General or an Admiral is what I really want to be
I'd like to be a General bold
But if it's true (as I've been told)
That Generals wear their spurs in bed
I'd be be an Admiral instead.
(On second thoughts, to be impartial
I might become an Air Chief Marshal.)

THE YAK

If a duck had a bark
And a dog had a quack
What short of noise would be made by a Yak?

THE 'DOWNWIND SKUNK'

In the brambly wood which grows near my house
Lived a respectable skunk and his spouse
Their dwelling was smart, had a fine front door bell
And the neighbours all called in spite of their smell.

Mrs Skunk liked her house to be clean and neat
And her husband remembered to wipe his feet
Except on that morning, that memorable dawn
When his first little son, skunk and heir was born.

This big bouncing skunklet was duly admired
By friends and relations until it transpired
It wasn't the drains of the house that were wrong
But that this young skunk smelt exceptionally strong

Though much as they loved him his fond parents felt
They could not escape from the fact that he smelt
His aroma was such that his dad and mum
Were both forced to admit to his noiseome hum.

They filled each of their rooms with freshly cut flowers
With strong eau de cologne and vase upon vase
Of sweet smelling herbs, but wherever they went
They could not escape from his powerful scent.

They built him a luxury nursery on wheels
And in it he slept, played and ate all his meals
This skunk creche they kept, except when it blew hard,
At a considerable distance to leeward.

His distinctive odour decreased as he grew
And now I don't think that he smells more than you
But although he's now old and his hair has thinned
His friends and relations still call him 'Downwind'.

STRANGE BUT TRUE

A Lur, a Lolo and a Kru
May sound absurd to me and you
But I assure you they exist
Like Zuni, Vu and Kababish
Macusi, Kubu and Pepo
Osyak, Nosu and Wadigo,

The Igabo and Igorot
The Hopi and the Hottentot
The Chewsures, Lazes and the Hare
All sound peculiar in our ear
But for sheer quaintness I commend
A Sart a Polab or a Wend,

The Kurds, the Hausa and Choctaw
Are names that we've all heard before
But have you ever heard of these
The Zapotecs and Waswazis
The Creeks, the Nupes and Bazibas
The Votyaks and the Budumas?

The Wolof and the Manobo
The Yezedi and the Jivaro
The Bubi, Mojo and the Jat
Are names that you may boggle at
But they are actual names and true
As Waziba and Mafulu.

Though Jambo and the Mangbettu
The Fon, the Funj, Orang Ulu
The Voguls, Thongas and Kipchaks
May your imagination tax
Don't let you choler rise and flush
With ire at tribes like Pschaws and Tush.

THE LITTLE ERS

By accident I learnt one day
A simple fact which I dare say
I should have realised before.
Most people don't read Fairy lore
And therefore they don't know about
A most select and special rout
Of little men who daily strive
To help us all to keep alive.

These little Ers (such is their name)
Are not in search of wealth or fame
(They're keen to work without reward
To stop themselves from being bored)
They're not at all like other elves
But eat the same food as ourselves
They like eclairs and good thick roux
Mince pies, blancmange and Irish stew.

They're not upstarts or nouveaux riches
But old as Time, and if you wish
I'll show you prehistoric rocks
Which clever men with snowy locks
Will say do prove beyond a doubt
That little Ers were round about
This earth before Time's dawn
(That's just before Grandma was born).

You seldom see these little men
When you have passed the age of ten
But even so Ers and their wives
Play quite a part in human lives.
If you would doubt the things I say
Think of the words you use each day
And you will find you read and speak
Of little Ers all through the week.

They turn their hand to anything
Singers are Ers who like to sing
Boilers to boil, makers to make
Bakers to bake the bread and cake
Thinkers are those who like to think
Tinkers are those who always tink
Stinkers are special Ers who, well
Have not a very pleasant smell.

The little Ers deserve renown
Both in the country and the town
The planters are the ones who plant
The food to feed your aged aunt
The printers are the Ers who print
Our money at the Royal Mint
And you there laughing up your sleeve
Doubters are those who don't believe

These Ers and many more beside
Inhabit town and countryside
But you will find some folk insist
That little Ers do not exist
Don't argue with these stubborn mules
(It's even worse to call them fools)
Just raise your hat, politely bow
And quote the verse which follows now.

Clinkers are not those naughty hordes
Of Ers in gaol, the warders wards
Brothers don't often make the broth
Mothers don't always have the moth
Suitors are not concerned with togs
Neuters do not resemble frogs.
These facts don't show that I'm a fool
But are exceptions to my rule.

LONDON STREETS

If you walked down London's streets with me
You would find (I'm sure that you'd agree)
There are many strange sights which I'll be bound
People miss, through keeping their eyes on the ground.

I've seen a polar bear in a bowler hat.

And sunlight reflected from Angkor Vat.

The fat boy from whom they make Lifebuoy soap
And Cardinal Puff who'd come straight from the Pope.

Yes I have. Really.

I've seen top hats of fustian, of treacle and tripe
Heard a popular song being sung by a snipe
Seen a Treasury man pouring gold down the drain
And a High Court Judge dancing jigs in the rain.
Yes I have. Really.

I've seen men with umbrellas of golden thread
(They usually have little horns on their head)
And horses with horse shoes made of peat
In order not to damage the street.
Yes I have. Really.

Yes I have. Really!

I've seen pigs in waistcoats of elegant cut
And seen the Lord Chancellor given a butt
By a well groomed goat of impeccable mien
Who didn't smell much and was tolerably clean.
Yes I have. Really.

There's only one sight that I seem to have missed
And I'm forced to believe that it doesn't exist
I haven't yet met it in eighty-five years
That's a child who washes behind the ears.

Do you think that bats
Ever hang with a frown

And wonder why

Everything's upside down?

THE MINK

If I was a Mink
I would sit and think
Why
If a Skunk has a stink
Has
Not a Mink
Got a stunk?

THE MAGIC EAST

Story books of Arabian nights
The Magic East, its strange delights
Tell of Sultans and Pashas and Viziers galore
But none that I've read tell of Abdul the Bore
Who told ten thousand tedious stories
To his least attractive Houris.

The other Sheikh the books omit
Is dear old Sulieman the Sit
Who spent an uneventful life
Entirely free from stress and strife
Resting his generous bottom on
A rather vulgar ottoman.

He was a harmless man and nice
And absolutely free from vice
Not like El Ramadam the Rude
Who tended to be rather lewd
And once spent eighty seven days
In a bumper hashish haze.

Omar the Munificent
Made sure he never spent a cent
That did not make a hundredfold
At minimum, so I've been told
His motto writ above his throne
Was Charity begins at home.

The Shah who really cut a rug
Was Akbar Khan who gave a hug
To everyone who passed his way.
Sometimes his hugging went astray
He hugged a her, an it, a him
On Holy days a Seraphim
His jewels were rare
His raiment fine
But sadly he drank too much wine
Provided by his Vizier shrewd
Who did his hugging in the nude.

THE VOYAGE

I sailed to the Island of Rantag Maru
In a big cricket bat made of old English yew
My hands were a motley lot to be sure
But very well versed in salt water lore
Our sail was a cloth of fine Maltese lace
Which took us along at a spanking pace

As we sailed to the Island of Rantag Maru
Where the Pipernicks howl
And the Happernogs prowl
The whole of the long night through

My mate was a mouse with a brown wrinkled face
Who lived on a diet of filletted plaice
He settled himself on the Top Gallant peak
And sang seafaring songs in a baritone squeak
Unless he was needed to shorten the sail
When he let himself down on the end of his tail.

My cook was a cat of ebony hue
Who served us with dishes of crickleshank stew
Hot muffsters and lobbins and fratterhogs beak
Langouste a la Reine and cold bubble and squeak
When he wasn't cooking he played on his flute
Whilst dishes were washed by a young galley newt

As we sailed to the Island of Rantag Maru.

My helmsman, a toad, smoked cheroots of old peel
And rumbled and croaked as he clung to the wheel
He'd an elegant wig powdered all over
With finest chalk from the white cliffs of Dover
And fashionable gloves which he wore on his fists
To match the impeccable lace at his wrists

As we sailed to the Island of Rantag Maru

When we were becalmed or the breeze wasn't strong
A Puff Pardon bird came and blew us along
(This bird is polite, hides his beak with his toes
And says 'Beg Your Pardon' whenever he blows)
he puffed all day long and so earned the right
to perch on the jackstaff all through the night

As we sailed to the Island of Rantag Maru,

When each sun went down and we wanted to sleep
An Ebbwank Dainty arose from the deep
And kept watch for us all through the hours of dark
With its luminous eyes which it lit with a spark
From its deep water tinder box small and frail
Which it kept in a rainproof pouch in its tail

As we sailed to the Island of Rantag Maru

We once got off course and were blinded with snow
When a Brontonag came and took us in tow
He seemed to be perfectly charming and gay
But he wanted, I think, to salt us away
And use us much later when all was quiet
As an agreeable change in his diet

As we sailed to the Island of Rantag Maru.

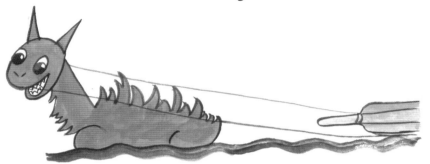

We couldn't escape and his cave came in sight
Just as we were all settling down for the night
Not expecting to see the very next dawn
But to be in his larder next to the brawn
Then a gallant Puff Pardon bird came to our aid
And dive bombed the monster with best marmalade

As we sailed to the Island of Rantag Maru

A brave Ebbwank Dainty who noticed our plight
Came up at full speed to join in the fight
With his spark he lighted a petrol soaked rag
And tried to set fire to the bad Brontonag
But missiles just bounced off his tough armoured skin
And he held on his course with a hungry grin

As we sailed to the Island of Rantag Maru.

This captor of ours was a giant carnivore
Who though he could multiply sixteen by four
Was not really clever but otherwise dull
Which made him preposterously easy to gull
When I got all my crew to stand upside down
He quietly turned turtle and started to drown

As we sailed to the Island of Rantag Maru.

We made good our escape and sailed on and on
Surrounded by snowstorms and fog all night long
The weather got colder as day followed night
And this seemed all wrong and not at all right
It should have got hotter as Rantag Maru
Is down in the south midst the sun and the blue

As we sailed to the Island of Rantag Maru.

I woke up one morning and found three small mice
(The mate's younger children) all covered in ice
The cook's splendid whiskers were heavy with frost
And these sights convinced me that we must be lost
I thought as I stared at the cold grey green foam
This weather is much like the winter at home!

As we sailed to the Island of Rantag Maru.

Indeed so it was for when land came in view
We found it was England, not Rantag Maru
I've not yet discovered how that came about
But am busy just now in refitting out
My old cricket bat, and I wonder if you
Would like to come with me as one of my crew

When I sail for the Island of Rantag Maru.

NEGLECTED

Goats have horns
Cows have cuds
Toes have corns
Soap has suds
Bodies have arms
Legs have feet
Farmers have farms
Bogs have peat
But I have nuffin – and nobody knows
That I'd very much like to have some clothes
For its awfully cold lying here in the hall
When you haven't got anything on at all
Its quite wrong to imagine that fur alone
Keeps a Teddy Bear warm when he's on his own.

A MODERN FABLE

In days of old (not long ago)
Lord Jeffrey drew his long yew bow
He shot his arrows in the air
And where they fell he did not care.
Later he moved from things of Bellum
To scratching dodgy words on vellum
And later still he took his leisure
Against his will at HM's pleasure
From time to time he was a vagrant
But all the while his wife stayed fragrant.

LAST THOUGHTS

If a stitch in time
Saves nine
Would a stitch too late
Save eight?

If an apple a day
Keeps the doctor away
What do you feed him
When you need him?

First published in 2005 by
Quillico Investments Ltd
P O Box 118
St Peter Port · Guernsey · GY1 3HA
Channel Islands
Email info@quillyco.com

ISBN 0 9551420 0 8
978 0 9551420 0 0

© Quillico Investments Ltd

Illustrations by Trudie Shannon
Prepared by Libanus Press, Marlborough
Printed by Butler & Tanner, Frome